Walker

Book

Belongs to:

_____

_____

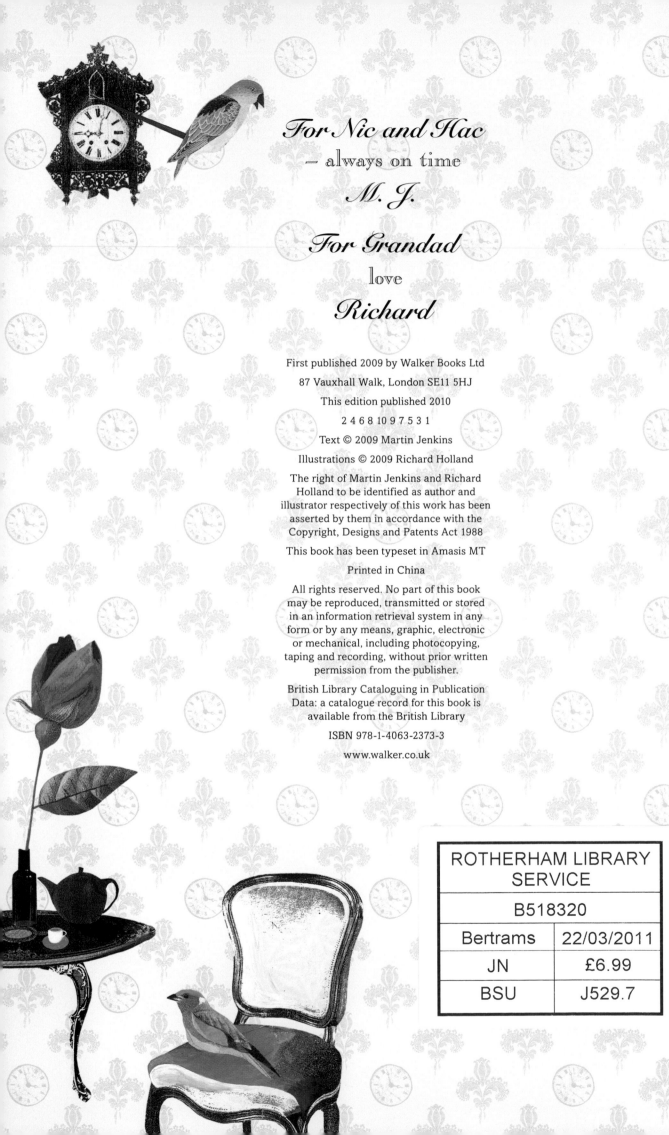

For Nic and Hac
– always on time
M. J.

For Grandad
love
Richard

First published 2009 by Walker Books Ltd

87 Vauxhall Walk, London SE11 5HJ

This edition published 2010

2 4 6 8 10 9 7 5 3 1

Text © 2009 Martin Jenkins

Illustrations © 2009 Richard Holland

The right of Martin Jenkins and Richard
Holland to be identified as author and
illustrator respectively of this work has been
asserted by them in accordance with the
Copyright, Designs and Patents Act 1988

This book has been typeset in Amasis MT

Printed in China

British Library Cataloguing in Publication
Data: a catalogue record for this book is
available from the British Library

ISBN 978-1-4063-2373-3

www.walker.co.uk

The
Time
Book

A

Brief History from

Lunar Calendars to Atomic Clocks

Written by *Martin Jenkins*

Illustrated by *Richard Holland*

Chapter One

Everybody knows time flies when you're having fun, and I'm sure we'd all agree that it drags when you're not.

But surely all time is the same, any minute is the same as any other minute – exactly 60 seconds long? And aren't minutes just a handy way of chopping up longer periods of time into nice, regular, bite-sized chunks? We all know there are 60 of them in an hour and 24 hours in a day, and seven days in a week. And if we do the sums, that means 10,080 minutes and 168 hours in a week. But that's a bit odd, isn't it? Why 10,080 minutes and not 10,000? After all, we humans normally like to be quite neat when it comes to ways of counting and measuring – 1,000 grammes in a kilogramme, 100 centimetres in a metre, that kind of thing.

Clock Riding
5 hour wait

i'm not having fun

We also generally like our measurements to stay the same – a centimetre is always ten millimetres, never nine or eleven. But time units aren't all like that. Take months. Some have 30 days, and some 31 and one, poor old February, only has 28. Except for every four years when it has 29. Well not quite every four years, because in most years that end in –00 (like 1800 and 1900) it only has 28 again, even though according to the four-year rule it ought to have 29. And then every 400 years it has 29 again (like in the year 2000). And all that means that years have 365 days, except when they have 366, which is every four years, except when it isn't. Confused? I'm not surprised.

So why are our ways of measuring time so wonky? Why are months and years not all the same length and why don't weeks divide neatly into months

Jan	Feb	Mar	Apr
31	28	31	30
May	Jun	Jul	Aug
31	30	31	31
Sep	Oct	Nov	Dec
30	31	30	31

and months into years? And come to that why are there 60 minutes in an hour, not 40, or 80 or ten, and why are there seven days in a week, and 365 (or so) days in a year?

And why are we so obsessed with counting and measuring and keeping time anyway? Why does it seem so important to know the exact time and date all the time? Was it always like this? Did people always get cross if you were two minutes late for class, or the dentist? 2,000 years ago would you have missed your trireme or your camel-train if you'd turned up at 11:01 instead of 10:59? If we didn't always live our lives by the clock, when did we start, and why?

And while we're at it, what is this stuff called time anyway?

Chapter Two

Humans are the only animals that have invented calendars and mechanical clocks but it seems that most, perhaps all, other living things have got ways of measuring time. We know this because virtually all of them do certain things at certain times, quite regularly. A lot of plants flower at only one time of year, whatever the weather, and many kinds of bird fly off in the autumn to warmer regions, leaving the places where they breed at almost exactly the same time year after year.

It might be that they're just reacting to changes going on around them – it gets cooler in the autumn and the days get shorter. And it's true that changes like these do often affect plants and animals. For example, you can fool a lot of plants into flowering at the wrong time of year by changing the temperature and giving them lots of extra light. But we now know it's not only to do with that. Experimenters have kept migrating birds for years on end in rooms cut off from the outside world, where the temperature never changes and with the same number of hours of light and dark each day. Still the birds try to migrate in autumn. And squirrels kept like this start to grow fat and sleepy in preparation for hibernation at around the same time that they would in the wild. Somehow they've kept track of the time through a whole year.

Some animals do even better than that. In North America there's an insect called a periodical cicada that lives for years and years as a larva underground, feeding on tree roots, before emerging one summer to breed. Some broods stay underground for 13 years and some for 17 years. The broods always get the number of years exactly right – they never pop up after 12 years, or 14 or 18. Somehow they can count off 13 or 17 years without making a mistake. We know that it's changes in the chemicals in the tree roots during spring that tell the larvae that a new year has arrived but we still don't understand how they know when the right number of years has passed.

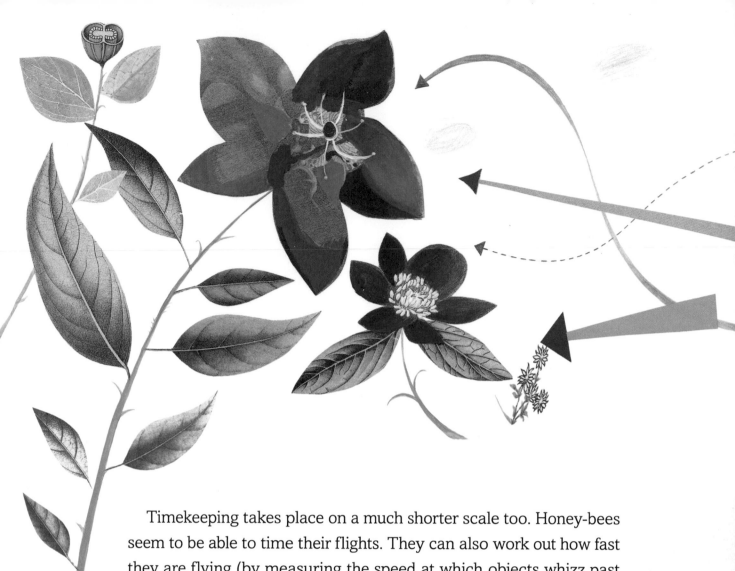

Timekeeping takes place on a much shorter scale too. Honey-bees seem to be able to time their flights. They can also work out how fast they are flying (by measuring the speed at which objects whizz past their eyes). They can combine these two things to work out how far from their hive a particular patch of flowers is. What's more they can tell all this to their hive-mates. When a scout bee finds a particularly good patch of flowers, she collects some pollen or nectar and zips back to her hive. Other bees cluster around while the bee performs a dance. If the flowers are nearby the bee just dances round in circles. But if they're more than 50 metres or so away, she performs a special waggle dance, running up and down the comb wagging her tail from side to side then circling round and starting again. The angle of her run up the comb tells the other bees which direction to go in relation to the sun – running straight up says "fly directly towards the sun" while running straight down means "fly directly away from the sun". The number of tail-waggings she does tells them how long they need to fly for at a particular speed to reach the flowers. The fewer wags in a dance, the longer it will take to reach the flowers. If there's a wind blowing in the wrong direction and it will take longer to reach a particular patch of flowers she performs fewer wags than if there is no wind.

You can also train bees to fly to certain spots at certain times of day by putting out food in those places at those times. Like the migrating birds and the hibernating squirrels they'll even do this if you keep them away from daylight. They've obviously got an internal clock that keeps track of the time of day.

Actually bees aren't the only ones with a daily clock: we all seem to have one – animals, plants, bacteria, fungi, you name it. Plants can be surprisingly regular timekeepers – just as some only flower at certain times of year, so some flowers open regularly at particular times of day. The great botanist Carl von Linne, who lived in Sweden in the eighteenth century, suggested making a floral clock by planting a bed with several different kinds of flowers and telling the time from which of them was open at that moment. He may never have grown a floral clock himself, but several people have done so since.

Carl von Linne

As for us humans, all sorts of things that our bodies do change regularly over the course of a day. Some are obvious – we usually get tired in the evening and hungry around three times a day. Others we don't notice so much, but they're still important. Our body temperature, for example, is at its lowest at around four in the morning and at its highest in the early evening. This affects how well we do different things – we seem to be better at exercising when our body temperature is at its highest, which may explain why athletes have often broken records when they run races in the evening.

These different daily rhythms are called "circadian rhythms" – circadian means "about a day" in Latin. They're driven by a clock inside us – actually not just one clock but millions and millions of them. It seems that all our cells contain molecular clocks, run by different genes being switched off and on in a particular order. These zillions of molecular clocks are kept in time with each other by a master clock which sits in the middle of the brain. It's tiny, much smaller than the head of a pin, but it's very important – if it's damaged, our timekeeping goes haywire. It works by sending out regular impulses that make sure that all the organs in the body are coordinated. It also receives nerve signals from the eyes telling it whether it's light or dark. This helps it keep time with the real time of day, as, if left to its own devices, it would run slow by a few minutes each day. It also means that our body clocks can adjust to changes in the length of day and night through the year and get over jet lag (eventually).

15

Chapter Three

So, if we humans are equipped with a perfectly good biological clock, why did our ancestors become obsessed with calendars and mechanical clocks? We'll never know for sure, nor do we know when people first began to make calendars and count off days and months and years. But it must have been around the time when humans first began to worry about the future and to think about how the world worked – why things happened when they did, and what made them happen.

Early humans would have noticed that the world around them was always changing, often in regular ways but sometimes in surprising ones. The most obvious regular change was from day to night and back again. Then there was the ebb and flow of the seasons. In tropical parts of the world there were rainy seasons alternating with dry seasons, while away from the equator, winter would give way to spring, followed by summer, then autumn and winter again. Animals and plants changed with the seasons – some birds would appear in spring and disappear in autumn, while trees would always flower and fruit and shed their leaves at particular times.

Those early humans must have noticed regular changes in the heavens too – the sun rose every day in the east and set every night in the west, and each night the great pattern of stars – the constellations – revolved in a circle around one point in the sky. The moon waxed and waned, and in summer the sun was above the horizon for much longer than in winter. The sun also rose and set in slightly different places each day, and reached a different height in the sky – in winter it would stay low over the horizon while in summer it would be overhead at midday. The constellations rose and set at slightly different times too.

But lots of irregular and unpredictable things happened too. Fierce storms might blow up, bringing deadly thunder and lightning, the rains could fail causing drought, or huge swarms of locusts might appear out of nowhere, devouring everything in sight. Mountains could suddenly explode into fire or start belching out poisonous fumes. In the skies a few of the brightest stars moved *very* oddly, shooting stars could sometimes be seen and even comets – strange lights that moved across the sky for nights on end. Very occasionally, part or even all of the sun or the moon went dark even when there were no clouds. When this happened to the sun it was as if night had come during the day.

Our early ancestors would have seen all this and tried to make sense of it. They decided there were gods and spirits everywhere who made pretty much everything happen. There were river gods, thunder gods and mountain gods. The stars and the sun and the moon might be gods, or places where gods lived. Some gods, like the sun god, were regular in their habits, while others, like the thunder god, were moody and unpredictable – but they evidently all had great power over human lives.

If you wanted to make sure that the right things happened in the future – that you would be victorious in battle or that the autumn storms would not destroy your homes – then you'd want to keep the gods happy. That would mean holding ceremonies for them, making offerings and sacrifices, often in particular sacred places at particular times.

If you were a farmer, your life might depend on the coming harvest being good, so you'd do everything you could to make sure that it happened. If you relied on regular floodwaters to fertilize your land, for example, you'd want to hold ceremonies for the gods who controlled the rivers before the flooding was due to happen, to make sure they were in a good mood. To work out when the floods were due, you'd need some sort of calendar.

Also, once you'd decided that the sun, moon and stars were important, you'd want to know what they were going to do in the future. Anyone who could know that would become a powerful person. Being able to predict dramatic events in the sky – like eclipses – would be incredibly impressive, a sure sign of having magical powers or being able to speak directly to the gods. Of course, if the rest of your tribe relied on you to know when things were going to happen it could be rather risky if you got things wrong – *not* predicting an eclipse, or a heavy flood, might have

21

Chapter Four

Setting
up a calendar
wouldn't be too
difficult. All you had to
do was take something that
seemed to happen regularly and
count off the number of days before
it happened again. The moon would be a
good place to start as it's very big and obvious in
the sky and changes over a short period. Watching the
moon and counting carefully, you'd quickly discover that a
new moon appeared every 29 days or so. So you could decide
to hold a ceremony on the fourth new moon from now and be able to
tell everyone how many days away that would be. But you'd soon find out
that a lunar calendar wouldn't keep very good track of the seasons, or match
what the other stars in the sky were doing.

A calendar that followed the seasons needed to be measured over a longer time, and as the seasons were obviously to do with the sun, one based on the sun would be sensible. Using a "gnomon" – a stick in the ground that cast a shadow – you could mark the length of the shadow at the time of day when it was at its shortest, that is, when the sun was at its highest point in the sky. The length of the shadow would change from day to day, growing gradually longer and then shorter again. By careful counting and with a lot of patience you would discover that the day when the shadow was at its shortest came around pretty much every 365 days. This was also the time when most of the stars would be back in their original positions in the sky.

So now you had a moon calendar for marking short periods of time, and a sun calendar for marking longer periods. Surely all you had to do was combine the two and you'd have one calendar for all your needs? But the trouble was, the two just didn't fit together. Trying to combine them caused the ancients a lot of headaches, and remember they didn't understand what was behind it all. Nowadays we do understand but it still hasn't helped us make a particularly logical calendar.

29 days

24 Hours......

So why *is* it so difficult to set up a regular calendar? It's all to do with the way the solar system works.

The earth is a planet spinning at an almost unchanging speed on its own axis (imagine a stick going through the middle of the earth from the north pole to the south pole). It takes almost exactly 24 hours for it to go round once and come back to where it started. And that, of course, is where our day comes from.

At the same time, the earth is rotating around the sun in a path called an "ellipse", like a slightly squashed circle. It takes almost exactly 365 and a quarter days to make one complete circuit – what our year is

365 Days and a bit

based on. The axis that the earth rotates around is tilted relative to the way the earth spins round the sun. That means that for half the year the northern half of the world leans towards the sun and the southern half leans away. During that time the days in the northern hemisphere are longer than the nights, while in the south the opposite is true. For the other half of the year the tilt has the opposite effect, and the nights in the northern hemisphere are longer than the days. Twice a year the days and nights in both hemispheres are exactly the same lengths. These are the equinoxes and in our calendar they fall on or around March 21st and September 21st.

old crescent

last quarter

waning gibbous

full moon

waxing gibbous

first quarter

new cresent

new moon

While the earth is going round the sun, the moon is going round the earth. It takes just over 29 and a half days to make one complete circuit, which is where we get our months from. Of course while the moon is going round the earth, the earth itself is still spinning once every 24 hours, and that is why the moon seems to rise and set like the sun and the stars. The moon doesn't produce its own light – what we see is the reflection of sunlight bouncing off its rocky surface. The phases of the moon, that is its regularly changing shape, are to do with the position of the earth, the moon and the sun and the amount of the sun's light that is reflected back to us from the moon.

Light from Sun

The stars that form the constellations are vast distances away and form an almost unchanging pattern in the sky, as though they were fixed in space. When we see them move through the sky it's because of the spinning earth, not because they are revolving around us.

The wandering stars are other planets like the Earth in our solar system. Five of them were known in the ancient world: Mercury, Venus, Mars, Jupiter and Saturn. Each is revolving around the sun in its own path and at its own speed. Mercury whizzes round in just 88 of our days, while Saturn takes 29 earth-years. Because their circuits don't match ours, they're always changing their position relative to the Earth. No wonder the ancient astronomers found them hard to keep track of.

Chapter Five

Given all this complication,
it's not surprising that so
many different calendars
have been developed.
The Mayans, who lived in Central America and
whose civilization was at its peak in around 600–
900, came up with one of the most extraordinary
calendars. They weren't very interested in technology
(they had the wheel once and seem to have given up
using it), but they were obsessed with time, numbers and
astronomy. Their months had just 20 days in them, and they
had two kinds of year, a sacred year of 13 months, or 260 days,
and a year based on the sun with 365 days. To set dates they
combined these to make a 52-year calendar, which they used to make
incredibly accurate astronomical predictions about the movements of
the planets – more accurate than anybody else could manage at the time.
The Mayans later developed another calendar that had a unit called
a "baktun" which was 144,000 days long. They believed that after a
great cycle of thirteen baktuns the world would be destroyed and recreated
again. Because their astronomical records were so precise, we can work out
that the most recent great cycle started on Wednesday 8th September 3114
BCE. This means that it – and, according to the Mayans, the world – will come
to an end on Sunday 23rd December 2012. Don't say you haven't been warned!

Don't need that!

The
Mayans
didn't pay
much attention to
the moon in developing
their calendar. This saved
them a lot of trouble, as it's
proved impossible to come up with
a regular calendar that combines the
movements of the sun and the moon and
doesn't need to be adjusted on a regular basis.
The Ancient Egyptians didn't even try. Instead they had
two separate calendars. One was a very practical calendar
for recording history (usually the great achievements of the
Pharaohs) and setting dates for the collection of taxes. It had 12 months
of 30 days with an extra five days at the end, making 365 days in all. However,
it quickly got out of time with the seasons as it didn't take into account the extra
quarter day in the real year. The other calendar, based on the moon, ran alongside
it, and was used to work out the dates of astronomical events and religious ceremonies.

32

f p ah dj d th t g k q sh s ch h h r n m f p

1_2 x 30 + 5

= 36_5

445

445

445

445

445

445

The Ancient Romans took the year to be 365 and a quarter days, but followed the moon in setting their months. They tried to keep things matched up by sticking in an extra short month every other year. If they'd done this sensibly they wouldn't have had much problem but the people in charge – called "pontiffs" – didn't behave themselves. They put in months of whatever length suited them – if they wanted to grab a few extra days of power they'd add a long month, if they wanted to speed up the time when a rival had to leave office they'd put in a short one. When Julius Caesar came to power in 51 BCE, the calendar was about three months out of time with the seasons and was generally in a terrible mess. So he decided to sort the whole thing out, with the help of a Greek astronomer called Sosigenes.

The calendar was reset. As a result, the year 46 BCE went on for an amazing 445 days instead of 365 – ever after known as "the year of confusion"! The new calendar started at the beginning of January 45 BCE, kept the normal year at 365 days and introduced a leap year of 366 days every fourth year. Every other month (January, March, May, July, September and November) had 31 days and the remainder had 30 except February, which had 29 days in normal years and 30 days in leap years.

With alternating long and short months, this scheme was neat and easy to remember although Caesar didn't have much time to enjoy it himself as he was assassinated the following year. But his efforts were commemorated by having the month Quintilius renamed in his honour as Julius (our July). Unfortunately his calendar was messed up some years later, in 7 BCE, apparently because the Emperor Augustus stole a day from February for the month he had named after himself (Augustus – our August). The lengths of September, October, November and December all had to be swapped around so as not to have three long months in a row. And that's why we have the odd system of days in the month that we use today.

Caesar's calendar – the Julian calendar as it was known – was taken up by the Christian church and spread throughout Europe. However, it wasn't quite correct. Caesar hadn't taken account of the fact that the true length of the year wasn't exactly 365 and a quarter days – it was eleven minutes (and fourteen seconds) shorter than this. Very, very slowly, the Julian calendar slipped out of time with the seasons. Midsummer day and the spring and autumn equinoxes moved forwards in the calendar by one day every 134 years. This was scarcely important during any one person's lifetime, but over the centuries the effect built up.

Nobody would have worried had it not been for the problem of when to have Easter, which was worked out from the timing of the spring equinox. As the spring equinox got earlier and earlier in the calendar, Easter sometimes fell much sooner in the year than people thought it should. Eventually, it was decided that something had to be done, and in 1582 Pope Gregory launched a new calendar.

It brought in the system of setting leap years that we use now – leaving one out at the start of most centuries. But just as Caesar had had to have one long year to correct the calendar in his time, so Gregory had to introduce a short year, to bring his calendar back in line with the seasons. The change wasn't as drastic this time round, but in the 1580s it still meant losing ten days somewhere.

Today is the
1st of January
Tomorrow
is the 12th
OK

Different places in Europe adopted the Gregorian calendar at different times. Italy, Portugal, Spain, France and Poland took it on straight away. Other countries, especially Protestant ones, were very suspicious of it, even though it made good astronomical sense. The Eastern Orthodox Churches still haven't accepted it.

Britain adopted the calendar in 1752. By this time 11 days not 10 had to be "lost" as the old Julian calendar Britain was still using had fallen even further behind the seasons. The days chosen were the 3rd to the 13th of September, which simply vanished. It must have been very strange, going to bed on the 2nd of September and waking up on the 14th! I'm sure you'd have been especially cross if your birthday had fallen in that period. Some people thought that 11 days of their life had been stolen from them and there are even said to have been riots about it.

The Gregorian calendar is now the most widely used civil calendar in the world, but there are still plenty of others in use, particularly religious ones, such as the Islamic calendar, which strictly follows the moon, and the Jewish calendar, which combines the moon and the sun. And there have been lots of attempts to simplify the calendar. In 1792 the French Revolutionary Parliament introduced one which, like the ancient Egyptian calendar, had twelve months of 30 days, with five days left over at the end (six in leap years). The months were divided into three "weeks" each ten days long and were given names that described them: the fourth month (which started on 21st December) was called "Nivose", meaning snowy, while the fifth month, which started on 20th January, was "Pluviose" or "rainy". This calendar didn't last very long, however, and on 1st January 1806 France went back to using the Gregorian calendar, like most of the rest of Europe.

Chapter Six

The ancient Assyrians attached great superstitious importance to the days when the moon changed phase – the 7th, 14th, 21st and 28th day after a new moon. These were unlucky days, and lots of activities, like preparing food or setting out on journeys, were forbidden. Instead time was devoted to making sure that the gods were happy. This is where the idea of a day a week of rest and worship comes from.

Each day in the seven-day cycle was associated with one of the main celestial bodies (the five known planets, the moon and the sun). The god or goddess linked to that body ruled over the day and offerings would be made to them. These old gods live on in our modern names for the days of the week. In English three of the names are directly linked to the names of the planets: Saturn's day, the Sun's day and the Moon's day. The other four days are named after Norse gods that were the equivalent of Roman planet-gods. Tuesday is Tiw's Day, the Norse version of Mars, the Roman god of war. Wednesday is Odin's or Wodin's day, who was linked to the Roman god, Mercury, Thursday is Thor's day, the god of thunder, who was Jupiter or Jove to the Romans, and Friday is Freia's day, the goddess of the home, who was the Norse equivalent of Venus, the Roman goddess of love. Other European languages stick more closely to the Roman. In French, for example, Tuesday is Mardi (Mars's day), Wednesday is Mercredi (Mercury's day), Thursday is Jeudi (Jove's day) and Friday is Vendredi (Venus's day).

Chapter Seven

Calendars deal with long periods of time, sometimes incredibly long ones. The champion of these must be the Indian calendar, which has a period called the kali-yuga that's 432,000 years long (the most recent kali-yuga started on Friday 18th February 3102 BCE, so it's still got quite a time to run). At the other end of the scale are the little units we divide our days into – hours, and minutes and seconds.

As far as we can tell the first people who measured short periods of time were the same people who developed calendars – astronomers or astronomer-priests. Because they wanted to keep detailed track of the movements of the stars, the moon and the sun, they needed to divide time into smaller divisions than just night and day. The ancient Egyptians were the first to divide the night-time into twelve parts, based on the time at which different groups of stars called "decans" rose above the horizon. To match the twelve night-time divisions they also divided the time between sunrise and sunset into twelve periods. Altogether, that made 24 periods, which is where our 24-hour day comes from.

Unlike our hours though, these Egyptian units weren't all the same length – during winter the night-time hours were longer than the day-time ones, while in the summer the opposite was true. Only at the equinoxes, when night and day were the same length, were all the hours the same. Astronomers found these changing hours ever more of a nuisance as their scientific calculations became more advanced. Finally, in around 150 BCE, Greek astronomers decided to make all hours the same length, whatever the time of year. They took up the system used by the Babylonians, which divided things into sixties, dividing their equal length hours into sixty "first-divisions", which we call "minutes", and then into sixty "second-divisions", which we still call "seconds".

The funny thing is, although they'd come up with a division as small as a second, they couldn't even measure minutes accurately – it would take another sixteen hundred years and a lot of ingenuity for that to happen.

43

The earliest time-measuring systems that we know about were invented by the Ancient Egyptians (them again) and were based on the sun during the day and the stars at night. The first sun-clocks were simple T-squares with lines marked on them that indicated the hours according to the length of the sun's shadow. Later, the Egyptians came up with primitive sundials, on which the time of day was shown by the direction of the sun's shadow rather than its length. At night they used an instrument like a plumb-line called a "merkhet". They could roughly tell the time by seeing where certain stars were between two merkhets.

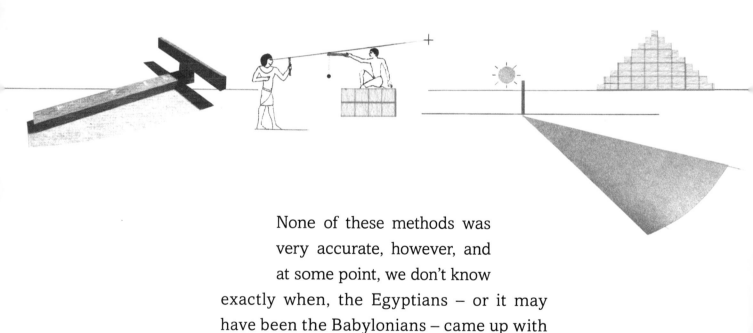

None of these methods was very accurate, however, and at some point, we don't know exactly when, the Egyptians – or it may have been the Babylonians – came up with a completely different way of measuring the time, using ... water! By arranging for a steady flow of water into and out of a container with horizontal lines marked on the side, you can measure the time by where the water level is in relation to the lines. It seems simple, but it wasn't because it's quite hard to keep water flowing steadily over a long period, and even the Egyptians couldn't get over the problem of having the clock sometimes freeze in winter!

The Ancient Greeks and the Romans took up the idea of the water clock, which they called a "clepsydra" and built some wonderfully elaborate and extravagant ones. Few people could afford their own – and those who could took great pride in showing them off, and in having a slave calling out the hours. But clepsydras did have some practical purposes too – like setting a limit to the length of speeches in the Roman Senate.

The most accurate water clocks in the ancient world were made not by Europeans, but by the Chinese. They had been using them since at least 600 BCE, but no one knows if they got the idea from the Babylonians or Egyptians, or if they invented them separately.

The most amazing and elaborate Chinese water clock was created by a man called Su Sung in 1088. It only lasted a few years before it was dismantled but luckily he had written a book in which he explained how the clock was made. In recent years several models of Su Sung's clock have been built, some of which can keep time to a minute a day, showing how accurate the original must have been.

In Europe during the Middle Ages people also relied on water clocks, as well as sundials, to tell the time. They haven't survived, but we're sure that none was as accurate or magnificent as Su Sung's. A couple of hundred years after Su Sung, though, something amazing happened in Europe that would totally change the way we think about time – the invention of the mechanical clock. It's a mystery exactly where and when this happened, but it was probably some time around 1280 and perhaps in England. We hardly know anything about the very first mechanical clocks, except that they must have been expensive, were usually installed in churches, and were almost certainly not at all accurate. The oldest we know much about was designed by Richard of Wallingford for the Abbey of St Albans in England in about 1328. It apparently didn't have a dial or hands, but instead marked the hours with a hammer that hit a bell. It operated with an ingenious device called a "verge-and-foliot escapement". This consisted of a bar (the foliot) that rotated backwards and forwards around a central rod (the verge) that controlled the way a toothed wheel turned. The wheel was driven by a weight suspended from a drum.

A craze for the new clocks swept through Europe. Clocks were designed and built that didn't just chime the hours but, like Su Sung's water clock, had moving models of the planets as well. The most famous of these was built by an Italian, Giovanni de Dondi, in Padua between 1348 and 1364. But they couldn't keep time precisely, constantly needed adjusting, and were hard to keep in good working order. Still, the new clocks had their uses (apart from showing off), mostly to call people to prayer and tell them when to start and stop working in towns and the surrounding fields.

Giovanni de Dondi

Chapter Eight

For the next couple of centuries, people depended on these not-very-accurate mechanical clocks and sundials to measure the passing of time. They also had the hourglass by now – it was invented at about the same time as the mechanical clock and was especially useful on ships as it worked perfectly well when bobbing up and down, unlike the new clocks.

During the fifteenth century someone came up with the idea of driving clockwork with a spring instead of a weight, which meant it was possible to build tiny clocks that could be carried about. And so the pocket watch was born. These new watches were masterpieces of miniaturization – but they still weren't very accurate.

Then, in the seventeenth century, things suddenly changed. Scientists like the Italian Galileo Galilei and the Frenchman Marin Mersenne discovered that pendulums made extremely good timekeepers. The first pendulum clock, built by the Dutch clockmaker Christiaan Huygens in 1656, could keep time to around ten seconds a day. By the end of the century, clocks that were accurate to half a second a day were quite common – though not _that_ common as they were very expensive and only the rich could afford them. At about the same time the invention of a new kind of spring, the "balance spring", did for watches what pendulums had done for normal-sized clocks.

Pendulum clocks became ever more precise in their timekeeping. A hundred years after Christiaan Huygens, the Englishman John Harrison made one that was accurate to a staggering one minute in ten years! Not only that but it kept time perfectly at sea, a truly amazing achievement, which helped solve one of the most important problems of the age: how a ship could work out how far east or west it had travelled on its voyage.

Chapter Nine

It wasn't until the twentieth century that timekeeping took another real leap forward. At the beginning of the century it was discovered that quartz crystals vibrated at a regular rate if an electric current was passed through them. The first quartz clocks were about the size of a wardrobe and weren't much better than the very best mechanical clocks – they kept time to around one second in five years. They soon improved, so that the best modern quartz clocks don't go out by more than a second in 275 years. Even that pales into insignificance compared with the next generation of clocks, which are based on the way that individual atoms vibrate. The latest versions of these are accurate to within one second in three million years.

Timepieces haven't just become hugely more accurate, they've become much smaller and cheaper too. You can buy a perfectly reliable quartz alarm clock or watch for the cost of a t-shirt or two. Not that you need to these days, as the time is everywhere – on mobile phones and computers, on the radio and on television, often fed directly to you from one of those atomic clocks that's correct to a billionth of a second. No excuse for being late for class or missing that train!

A hundred years ago it wasn't like this at all. Although clocks and watches were by no means rare, they were still expensive luxuries for working people, who mostly relied on the town-hall clock, the station clock, or the factory hooter to tell them the time. A hundred years before that there wasn't even an agreed time to tell: towns and cities stuck to their own time, which was generally the one on the clock of the most important church in town. Twelve noon by the clock in Bristol might be 15 minutes later than 12 noon in London. It didn't really matter – it would take at least 12 hours to travel by the fastest stagecoach from one to the other, so a few minutes here or there made no difference, and no one got upset if you were ten minutes or half an hour late for a meeting.

1 o'clock

2 o'clock

3 o'clock

The railways
changed all that. Trains ran
to strict timetables, they wouldn't wait for
anyone and they could whisk you from one town to
another at a speed undreamt of just a few years earlier.
It became important that people were punctual and that everyone
knew what the time was wherever they were. Britain, where the railways
were first developed, became the first country to standardize its time. The
time kept by the Royal Observatory in Greenwich, near London, was chosen,
and by 1855 nearly all the public clocks in the country were set to it. A timekeeping
signal was transmitted across the country through electric cables laid along the
railway tracks. Other countries gradually followed suit in sorting out their time.

Platform *1*

London
Waterloo

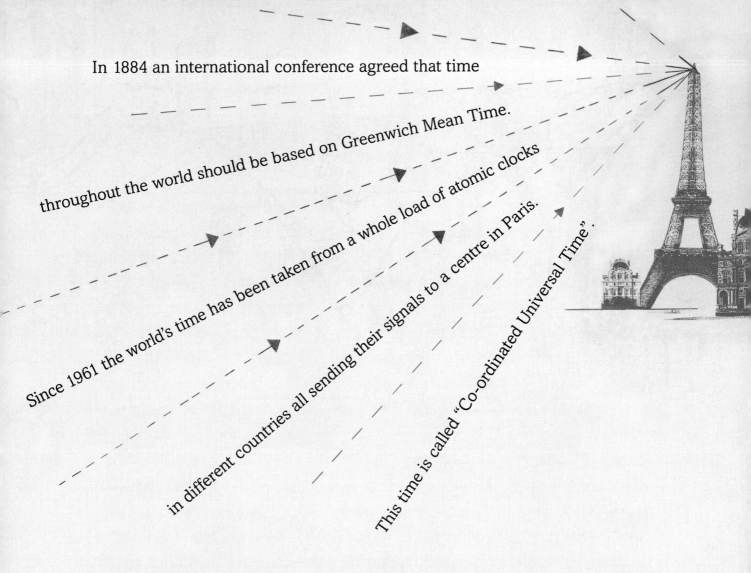

In 1884 an international conference agreed that time

throughout the world should be based on Greenwich Mean Time.

Since 1961 the world's time has been taken from a whole load of atomic clocks

in different countries all sending their signals to a centre in Paris.

This time is called "Co-ordinated Universal Time".

So now here we are with a time that all the world agrees on, accurate to a thousand-millionth of a second. And we know exactly how long it takes for the earth to spin once round its centre and for the earth to go round the sun. We've even got a pretty good idea how many years old the universe is (about 13.7 billion at the last count). It seems as if we've got it sorted. But despite all this do we really understand time at all?

Chapter Ten

Well, it seems the more we find out about time, the stranger it becomes. A hundred years ago Albert Einstein showed that time didn't necessarily run at the same speed for everyone – it could stretch out or shrink depending on how fast you were moving. He called this his theory of relativity. You can only notice a difference when you're travelling very fast indeed – nearly at the speed of light (30,000 kilometres a second). We humans can't travel at anything like that speed but we can see the effect of relativity by looking at the tracks left by minuscule, sub-atomic particles called "mu-mesons".

If we *could* travel incredibly fast in spaceships (and it's certainly not a complete impossibility), then some very odd things would happen. Imagine a pair of twins, one, an adventurous astronaut and the other a stay-at-home. The astronaut sets out in a spaceship travelling at about 25,000 kilometres a second to visit the nearest star to earth, which is around four light years away (about 40,000,000,000,000 kilometres), then whizzes home again. According to the clock on the spaceship, the round-trip takes about five years, which means the astronaut is five years older when she gets back to earth. But back on earth, *ten* years have gone by, so her twin is ten years older than when she waved the spaceship off – she's aged twice as fast as her space-travelling sister. It's weird but it's true.

There are other ideas about time that we're less sure about. Some people believe it's made up of tiny particles, far far smaller than an atom, that can't be divided into smaller pieces. Others that it's part of the bits of string that they believe make up the universe. Then there's the possibility that one day the universe will stop expanding and start to shrink back in on itself, and time will run backwards, so we'll all get younger and younger rather than older.

I don't know about any of that, but I still think time flies
when you're having fun and drags when you're not,
and on that I'm sure we're all agreed.

Nearest Star

40,000,000,000,000 Kilometres

25,000 Kilometres a second

Index

More excellent non-fiction from Walker Books

ISBN 978-1-4063-1972-9

ISBN 978-1-4063-2180-7

ISBN 978-1-84428-737-6

ISBN 978-1-4063-2222-4

ISBN 978-1-4063-1929-3

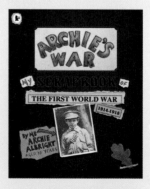

ISBN 978-1-4063-1002-3

Available from all good bookstores

www.walker.co.uk